T0171465

Free Indeed

Chaplain Larry Briggs

WestBow
PRESS
A DIVISION OF THOMAS NELSON

WestBow Press books may be ordered through booksellers or by contacting:

WestBow Press
A Division of Thomas Nelson
1663 Liberty Drive
Bloomington, IN 47403
www.westbowpress.com
1-(866) 928-1240

Because of the dynamic nature of the Internet, any web addresses or links contained in this book may have changed since publication and may no longer be valid. The views expressed in this work are solely those of the author and do not necessarily reflect the views of the publisher, and the publisher hereby disclaims any responsibility for them.

Any people depicted in stock imagery provided by Thinkstock are models, and such images are being used for illustrative purposes only.

Certain stock imagery © Thinkstock.

ISBN: 978-1-4497-7021-1 (sc)
ISBN: 978-1-4497-7023-5 (hc)
ISBN: 978-1-4497-7022-8 (e)

Library of Congress Control Number: 2012923215

Printed in the United States of America

WestBow Press rev. date: 12/13/2012

Contents

Preface

Before we get started, I would like to take a few minutes to share my heart and why I think this book is needed, especially in the interesting but critical times in which we are now living.

The concept and focus of this writing was birthed in my heart in February of 2005. At that time I had been employed at the Riverside Regional Jail in Hopewell, Virginia, for almost a year. I was initially employed as a Case Manager and then presented with the opportunity to assume the position of Chaplain / Faith-Based Programs Manager.

Working daily now for over eight years in this environment has opened my eyes and heart to the epidemic of crime in America and the horrible consequences it has on both the criminals and their victims. Most of our correctional facilities are underfunded, understaffed, and in dire need of renovated and/or new facilities to secure the inmate population they are required to service. At Riverside, where I am privileged to minister, our facilities are modern, exceptionally clean, and managed by a top-notch staff. Even with these assets our stress level is very high as we seek to house and provide care for a daily average of thirteen hundred inmates. It takes an incredible amount of time, talent, and finances for the sworn staff to maintain security and a safe environment for both the inmate population and our staff. This is true in any jail or prison, and the average citizen has no concept what it is really like on the inside. I have developed such a high respect for correctional officers who work every day on the front line, the civilian staff who provide much-needed programs and support, and most of all, the command staff and administrators who are responsible for the overall management of these facilities. They need and deserve our daily prayers.

It is very easy, even as Christians, to develop a mind-set that the criminal mind cannot be rehabilitated. At best, let's incarcerate them and keep them for long periods of time in less than adequate institutions, for the protection of mainstream society. However, my firsthand experience during these past eight years has taught me to think differently. I believe that there is fundamentally good in all people and with the right nurturing partnered with a sincere demonstration of God's powerful love, the hardest heart and the most criminally minded can be changed. It requires the work of the Holy Spirit through committed servants who are willing to take the risk and invest the time. I can recount numerous occasions when inmates, both male and female, sat in my office or a cold, stuffy jail cell (many who were guilty of such horrid crimes that I would be uncomfortable putting them in print), weeping in sincere repentance, after having come to the truth from reading a Bible donated by a local church or group that was given with a kind word and sincere prayer, in a nonjudgmental spirit. One thing that I have definitely learned is that prison doors, however secure, cannot keep out the Spirit of God. The power of His love can penetrate even the darkest cell in the maximum security unit, changing the heart and life of the worst among the worst. I am reminded every day that Jesus died on the cross for these inmates, just as He did for me.

Eight years ago, as I was walking to my job interview at Riverside Regional Jail, the Holy Spirit whispered a powerful focus statement that has become an anchor in my life and ministry. He said, "I am not planting you in this place to convince people that they are wrong, but rather, to *show* them that Jesus is right." It is with this mandate that I embrace the task of putting into print the truths that the Holy Spirit has deposited into my heart and mind for those who are in bondage. One of the realities of our present culture is the fact that for every incarcerated inmate in America, there are hundreds, perhaps thousands, of others on the outside living in self-made prisons with invisible bars of destructive habits and addictions. And we need to get real and be totally honest: Many who claim the name of Jesus, attend church on a regular basis, and believe the fundamental teaching of the Bible are among them. We live in an addictive society, and many live (exist) every day in life-destroying bondage. We all need help, and, unfortunately, the help we need cannot be found on the psychologist's couch, nor in a pill bottle, or even a two-hour service on Sunday morning. These things might help but we need so much more.

I believe that the truths, insights, and principles shared in this book can bring freedom to anyone in bondage to anything, if adhered to and sincerely sought after.

It is my most earnest and fervent prayer that our heavenly Father will use this work to penetrate jails and prison cells all across our great nation and, more importantly, the hearts and minds of all who read it who are sincerely seeking positive change through true freedom. I passionately believe that Jesus is the truth, the way, and the life and that the *truth* will set you free.

And when the *Son* sets you free, you will be *free indeed*!

"For I know the plans I have for you," says the Lord. "They are plans for good and not for disaster, to give you a future and a hope." (Jer. 29:11 NLT)

Therefore if any man be in Christ, he is a new creature: old things are passed away; behold, all things have become new.

(2 Cor. 5:17 KJV)

I am crucified with Christ: nevertheless I live; yet not I, but Christ liveth in me. And the life that I now live in the flesh, I live by the faith of the Son of God, who loved me and gave Himself for me. (Gal. 2:20 KJV)

I ask the Father in his great glory to give you the power to be strong inwardly through his Spirit. I pray that Christ will live in your hearts by faith and that your life will be strong in love and be built on love. (Eph. 3:16–17 NCV)

CHANGE!

If you always think what you've always thought, then you will always feel what you've always felt.

If you always feel what you've always felt, then you will always do what you've always done.

If you always do what you've always done, then you will always get what you've always gotten.

If you always get what you've always gotten, then you will always think what you've always thought!

Author Unknown

Syllabus / Mapping Our Journey

(A Journey into Self-Evaluation)

The Psychology of Change

Why Am I Who I Am?

Why Do I Do What I Do?

Cultivating Positive Change!

Decisions Have Consequences

Deciding My Destiny / Taking "Ownership" of My Life

"Responding" Not "Reacting"

Developing a Decision-Making Plan

Cultivating Lasting Relationships

Understanding Your Basic Needs

The Four Levels of Intimacy

"Growing" Positive Relationships

Introduction

The pathway into self-evaluation is a personal journey that has the potential of *changing* your life forever. The truths that we share in this personal workshop are solid biblical principles presented through a psychological perspective. Our heavenly Father created each of us with a soul, a spirit, and a body. Most of our attention is focused on the physical because we are driven by human instinct, which is birthed from the five senses: touch, sight, hearing, taste, and smell. However, we need to understand that each of these feelings is interwoven into our emotional (spirit) being, and what we feel and what we do is greatly influenced by our psyche (spirit and soul). *The reality of life is that we do what we do because of how we feel, and how we feel is determined by the way we think. Therefore, positive change can only take place as we learn how to change how we think, which will result in managing how we feel, thus changing how we act.*

The prevailing philosophy of modern psychology is that our psyche (spiritual being) is predetermined by genetics, environment, and the individual influences into which we are born. The end result is a generation living with the belief that we are who we are, and in order to experience any similitude of peace and harmony, we must accept who we are and learn to live within the perimeter of our unalterable personality. In simple terms, we cannot change who and what we are. I do not believe that. I am convinced through personal experience and a lifetime of study in God's Word, the Bible, that we *can* change how we feel, thus changing how we live. If we are willing, with an open heart and a teachable spirit, to confront the destructive issues in our lives, God will enable us by the power of His Holy Spirit to not only overcome them but also to control the way we think, which will help us manage our feelings and then change how we act.

As we embark on this exciting personal journey of self-evaluation, I would like to encourage you to take a few moments to properly prepare yourself so that you will receive the maximum benefits from this spiritual workshop. In order to clearly understand these truths, you need to quiet yourself before your heavenly Father, get in neutral gear, and prayerfully ask God to deposit His life-freeing principles into your heart and spirit. What I mean by "neutral gear" is a place where physically and emotionally you can maintain an open heart and a receptive mind. Understand that along this path into self-discovery you will begin to see the real you, and sometimes that can be very painful. But remember that pain can be a wonderful motivator for change when change is needed. Periodically remind yourself that God is greater than any problem that you have and that He will partner with you in your determination to discover His destiny for your life. He has always loved you. There is nothing that you have done or could do to change this wonderful truth. As you come to understand the biblical revelation of *grace,* His love will become your motivation for every thought and deed, and as you begin to walk in this truth, you will come to know what Peter meant when he taught that "love covers a multitude of sins" (1 Peter 4:8). His love will change your attitude and your activities.

I'm excited for you, and I pray that you share my enthusiasm as you begin this life-changing journey. So get ready, buckle up, and enjoy the trip into understanding that the *influence of character* does count and that *you can* become the person that God made you to be, the person that you want to become.

Getting Started

Planning and preparation are the key essentials to a successful trip. As you embark on this journey into *change*, I would like to suggest a plan for study that will enable you to reach your intended goal.

The first step is to examine your life and heart before God and make sure that your relationship with your heavenly Father is growing more intimate each day. Prayerfully seek Him and allow Him to search your heart, and be willing to accept the truth that can set you free. Ask the Holy Spirit to reveal to you any attitude or activity in your life with which He is not pleased. Be willing to place whatever God shows you at the altar of your heart and ask your Father to give you the wisdom and strength to walk away from it. Your relationship with God is the most important issue in your life, and if it is not what it should be, nothing else in your life will work out right.

Next, I encourage setting a specific time each day for personal fellowship with God through prayer, meditation, and Bible study. The amount of time is not so much an issue as is the discipline of having a personal time with Him each day. He desires to meet with you, and it is in this secret place where your relationship with your heavenly Father becomes intimate and personal. Learn to make personal worship a priority. You will be amazed at the difference it will make in how you view life and all of its challenges.

Next, you need to develop a plan of study. Are you entering this journey as a personal study, or will you be participating in a group study facilitated by a trusted teacher? Whether you are working on a personal basis or in a group, make sure that you have the necessary tools to complete the workshop: a Bible, notebook and pen, the workbook, and a quiet place that is free from distraction. Set a specific time period for your study and schedule the same time each day for the next six days. Most importantly, cultivate an open heart and ready mind so that you can receive what the Holy Spirit will deposit into your spirit. Don't shy away from the pain of truth but embrace it, allow the Holy Spirit freedom to change you into His image and to place within you the mind of Christ.

Finally, don't rush through just to complete the workshop. Pace yourself, be patient, and give yourself time to pray and meditate on the truths that you will encounter in each study session. I suggest that you focus on one chapter a day, and allow time at the beginning of each day to review and evaluate the former day of study. Again, let me encourage you to think deeply and allow the Holy Spirit to teach you how to apply what He deposits into your heart to your daily life. Don't resist *change,* but rather pursue it with the understanding that you are becoming a new person made into His image (2 Cor. 5:17).

And he taught in their synagogues, being glorified by all …

"The Spirit of the Lord is upon Me, because he has anointed Me to preach the gospel to the poor; he has sent Me to heal the brokenhearted, to proclaim liberty to the captives and recovery of sight to the blind, to set at liberty those who are oppressed; to proclaim the acceptable year of the Lord." And He began to say to them, "Today this Scripture is fulfilled in your hearing." (Luke 4:15, 18, 19, 21 NKJ)

The Psychology of Change

The Scriptures teach that Jesus came to heal all who were oppressed. He brought spiritual, physical, and emotional healing. As you begin the first phase of your journey into self-discovery, I would like to encourage you to pause for a moment and look clearly at your life as it is today. If you are like most of us, you will have to admit that life has brought you many disappointments and possibly some deep hurts. The word that Jesus used in the above text for *oppressed* is better understood by using the word *bruised*. Many of us are walking around performing our daily duties while nurturing deep bruises that we have received from negative life experiences. Perhaps your bruises came from the tragic death of a loved one, an unexpected layoff, the loss of a friendship, a failed marriage, or any one of an endless list of events that we encounter in everyday life. Pain is something that *all* of us have in common, and if you are not hurting right now, brace yourself, because you will. This is not a negative confession but the reality of life, as we know it. None of us are strangers to tears. From Adam's days until now, heaven has been consistently bombarded with the wailing cries of the brokenhearted.

The real issue is not when or how we will experience hurt but how will we respond to it. Medical science has made remarkable advances in addressing our physical hurts and diseases, but only Jesus can heal a broken heart and wounded spirit. Psychologists can evaluate, analyze, and help us identify our emotional and mental needs, but at best, they can only diagnose the problem and prescribe powerful mind-altering drugs to help us cope. Jesus is the *only* one who can heal and deliver.

The pathway into self-discovery that leads us to this place of wonderful healing begins with self-examination that reveals what hurts and bruises we are carrying around. I want you to ask yourself three major questions: *Why am I who I am? Why do I feel the way I feel? Why do I do what I do?* Prayerfully consider each of these questions. As you individualize and identify your bruises, search for the root cause and then you will know what you need to bring to the altar.

You cannot ignore your bruises; if unattended they will turn into stress fractures that will ultimately destroy your self-esteem. For the purpose of this workshop, I define *self-esteem* as being how you perceive yourself determined by your understanding of how others view you. Simply put, you will always view yourself through the opinion of others around you. You can say that you don't care how others feel about you, but the truth is you really do. We have been created with an intricate need to love and be loved. When we are betrayed, ignored, or disappointed by someone who we consider to be a friend, it creates a bruise in our spirit. If unattended it will create a cancer in our emotions that will result in a fractured self-esteem. It becomes more devastating and complex when the friendship/relationship is lost due to our own actions and/or poor decisions. *As hard as we may try, we cannot help but to see ourselves the way we think others see us.*

This brings us to our first critical crossroad on our journey to becoming the person we want to be, the person that our heavenly Father designed us to become. We have to acknowledge our need for *change*, identify our bruises, and seek the healing touch of Jesus in order to change. At this crossroad we will either continue in the path that we have always walked or we will turn to the cross for healing and deliverance. Please take a moment and re-read the syllogism titled **C H A N G E** in the Introduction to the book. Think about the truth that it presents. Are you living in an emotional rut? Like the children of Israel, are you walking around in an endless circle always thinking the same thing, always feeling the same feelings, always getting the same stuff? Think deeply about the major hurts and disappointments that you have experienced in your life. Painful experiences in life will either make you *bitter* or they will make you *better*. The end result is determined by your personal decision as to which road you will travel. If you will confront your bitterness and anger with a prayerful heart, you will begin to see that the road you've chosen to walk is no one's fault but your own. You may truly be a victim; you may have been misjudged, falsely accused, and wrongfully convicted. But how you respond ultimately determines where you will end up. Let me state the central truth to this study again: *The reality of life is that we do what we do because of how we feel and how we feel is determined by the way we think. Therefore, positive change can only take place as we learn how to control how we think and feel.* Here's the good news: God through the power of His Holy Spirit will not only bring healing to your self-esteem but He will also enable you to overcome negative thinking and help you control your feelings, which will change how you live. He can heal your fractured self-esteem if you are willing to change directions and turn to the right, to the way of the cross. It's *your* decision that will determine your destiny.

As you stand at this critical crossroad, let me share with you a definitive plan that involves four steps to recovery and healing. In order for positive change to occur, there must be first a genuine *desire* to change. In my pastoral and counseling ministry I have encountered many people who were sick and tired of always being victimized and coming up short. They expressed a deep hatred for life as it is and a self-justified anger at the people and circumstances that contributed to their misery. They walked around with the needless baggage of resentfulness, blindly believing that things encumbering them never would change.

Does this sound familiar? With this attitude people become prisoners of what I call "a victim's mentality." They are quick to judge others and make no apology for blaming their situation on everyone and everything else. The truth of the matter is that no person, government, agency, or circumstance can imprison you unless you decide to let it happen. Life is not always fair and sometimes it downright stinks, but we determine the outcome. In every situation of life you must choose to *react* or *respond* (more on this in the next chapter). When I fully understand that most of my actions are birthed in my attitude about life, then I can focus on the real issues and take control of my life by allowing the Holy Spirit to change my attitude. I must cultivate right thinking, and this begins with a sincere *desire* to change—not my circumstances, but to change *me* so that I can respond properly to situations I encounter in life.

One of the numerous facts of life that I have learned these many years in ministry is that normally most people get whatever they truly desire. If we really want something, regardless of how difficult it may be, we will find a way to attain it. The stubbornness and strength of the human spirit is both a liability and an asset. The drug addict will always find a way to get his or her fix. The alcoholic will always find a way to the bottle. The nicotine addict will always find a way to justify smoking, and the food addict will always find an excuse for the third and fourth trip to the buffet bar. The sex addict will always justify his or her perverted behavior, and even convince himself or herself that they are "normal," that there is nothing wrong with his or her lifestyle. The power-hungry executive will always find a way to the top regardless of whom he hurts in the process.

In psychology there is a principle that every counselor works with: Until the *pain* of an individual's destructive habits outweigh the *gain*, change will never take place. Unfortunately that has proven to be true in many lives, even those of us who are believers in Jesus. Our feelings overrule our faith, and we live as victims rather than as the victors the Father through Jesus has made us. In order to find healing, I urge you to confront your wrong thinking, come to the cross, and ask God to cleanse you and to create within you a pure heart.

Jesus taught that true happiness comes to those who are hungry for righteousness. What you hunger for is what you will seek. Be honest with yourself, and most importantly be honest with God. Admit your sinful desires, repent, and allow the Holy Spirit to renew your mind. Pray specifically that He will create in you a sincere desire to change then cultivate that desire through prayer, meditation, and Bible study. Get involved in a local church that can foster your spiritual growth, and draw strength from the fellowship with your faith-specific community. Renounce sinful habits and wrong thinking and stay close to the cross. You will be amazed how quickly your desires will change and how differently you will begin to feel.

Desire is a strong motivator in our lives. If our desire is pure before God, we will hunger for righteousness in every area of our life.

However, desire alone will not produce lasting change. We are all creatures of habit, and regardless of how strong our desire for change may become, too often we revert back to the same old destructive habits, and in so doing become more addicted than before. I am a firm believer in the saving power of God, but I also believe in the mystery of free will. Father will not force us to seek Him and to live by His precepts; therefore, *desire* must be reinforced with *decision.* While cultivating a desire for change is an all-important first step, the second is equally important. We must make a confirmed decision to change our way of thinking and how we live. Learning how to make good decisions will be the focus of the next chapter, but here I need to emphasize the necessity of making up your mind that you are going to change. Without a *decision* to change, you never will.

Desire can produce a decision, but we need to understand that our decisions must be strong enough to cause us to follow through on what we desire. In other words, I have to make up my mind to change if change is to ever happen in my life. A decision is simply weighing all my options and choosing the one that is most profitable in any given situation.

As we will discuss in the next chapter, most of us make decisions based on how we feel. That's why we must see the connection between desire and decision. We come to a point in every battle where we have to decide which way to go. We have been born again through the power and grace of the cross, but that does not rob us of our free will. Father gives us the privilege and the responsibility to choose. Every day I am confronted with choices that will affect my relationship with God, my family, and others.

When Joshua was appointed the leader of Israel after the death of Moses, he learned this very important unchanging life principle. During a time of intense battle he laid it out as plain as it could be stated. He declared to a floundering people who had spent forty years wandering in the desert, "Today, I set before you a blessing and a curse ... choose who you will serve. As for me and my house, we will serve the Lord" (Joshua 24:15, author's paraphrase). If you are to be free from the destructive habits that control you, you must make a decision to be free.

Once you have made your decision, then it's time to embrace the third step—*discipline*. The very word creates an uncomfortable feeling in our thinking. As members of the microwave culture, we have come to believe that we are entitled to anything we desire and to have it now. We need to understand that the principles that influence this culture are in direct opposition to the principles that govern the kingdom of God. Jesus' teachings were not only rejected by the religious hierarchy of His day but in the end they caused Him to be crucified.

It's no different today. We are much more sophisticated in our lifestyles and we enjoy personal pleasures and a life made easy by unbelievable technology, but the end result is the same. If we sow according to the flesh, we will reap what the flesh produces. If we live according to the Spirit, we will receive from the Spirit fruit that produces abundance in every area of our lives.

It is interesting to note that self-control (discipline) is a fruit of the Spirit. Paul taught in the book of Romans that the battle between the flesh and the spirit never ceases. However, he emphatically states that we *can* win the war through the power of God's indwelling Spirit. The only way we can conquer the lusts of our carnal nature is to be reborn and daily submit to the lordship of Christ through the power of His Spirit in us. Out of a pure *desire* we can be motivated to make the right *decision*, but without *discipline* we will fail. Paul gives us the three "keys" of a disciplined life in Romans 8 and 12: submission, surrender, and sacrifice.

The final step toward a positive change that will result in the healing of your fractured self-esteem is *determination*. Each of these four steps is necessary for a successful journey. I don't know that I would say that any one step is more important than the others, but I cannot overstate the importance of determination. Life is becoming more difficult and complex, and in most cases emotional healing is a work in progress rather than instantaneous. There is no doubt that God can and does sometimes heal instantly and completely. However, it has been my experience that emotional healing and mental healing occur gradually over a period of time. I have come to believe that Father has a purpose in the process of healing over a period of time. It gives us time to process the change and to make the transition from a wounded soldier to a formidable member of God's great army. Discipline is the means by which we develop good and strong habits that can last only with a spirit of determination.

On this journey you will encounter many obstacles and numerous potholes. Inevitability you will slip and fall. When you do, remind yourself that Jesus is your best friend and that He is walking this journey with you—and He will be there to pick you up. Whatever you do, don't give up. God not only destines you for a particular pathway but He has also empowered you by His Spirit to finish the course.

Don't become distracted through discouragement but rather develop a strong determination to become the person you want to be, the person He has designed you to become. Determination will help you to keep going, and it will give you the strength to navigate the rough places successfully. Determination is a matter of the mind, not the body. You will grow tried and weary both physically and emotionally and there will be plenty of opportunities to quit. But determination partnered with the power of the Holy Spirit working within you will keep you focused and moving forward.

In summary, let me state again that *change* is not only necessary, but with God it is possible. If you cultivate a pure *desire* for change and are willing to make the right *decisions* to change then develop self-*discipline* through an undaunted *determination*, you will soon become a victor rather than a victim.

Session 1
Journal Worksheet

1. Write our focus Scripture for phase one of your journey.

_____

_____

_____

_____

_____

_____

_____

_____

_____

2. The word oppressed is best understood by using the word:

_____

_____

_____

_____

_____

_____

_____

3. List five things that may create a bruise in our hearts (spirit).

1. _____
   _____

2. _____
   _____

3. _____
   _____

4. _____
   _____

5. _____
   _____

4. Define self-esteem.

_____
_____
_____
_____
_____
_____
_____

5. What is the central truth of this study?

_____

_____

_____

_____

_____

_____

_____

_____

6. List the four steps to *CHANGE*, giving a brief summary of each one.

1. _____ =

_____

_____

_____

_____

2. _____ =

_____

_____

_____

_____

3. _____ =

_____

_____

_____

_____

4. _____ =

_____

_____

_____

_____

7. Personal reflection/prayer focus: What is the biggest challenge that you are facing in order to *change*?

_____

_____

_____

_____

_____

_____

_____

_____

_____

Thousands upon thousands are waiting in the valley of decision.
(Joel 3:14 NLT)

"But if you are unwilling to serve the Lord, then choose today whom you will serve ... But as for me and my family, we will serve the Lord."

(Joshua 24:15 NLT)

Decisions Have Consequences

Now that you have successfully navigated the first crossroad by confronting the need for change in your life, let's continue down this road to freedom with a renewed mind and spirit, knowing that our Father God is with us when we walk in His truth; indeed, no weapon formed against us can prosper (Isa. 54:17).

Our next stop will be in the place that the prophet Joel called, "the valley of decision." We learned in the previous chapter that *decision* is one of the four critical steps to recovery and victory. Learning how to make good decisions is one of the most important life skills that we can acquire. Your destiny and the quality of your life are determined by your personal decision-making process. Here is a life principle that we must embrace and understand:

Decisions have consequences! Every day we have to make decisions and whether they are routine or significant, each decision will affect our relationship with God, family, career and life as a whole. Our Heavenly Father has a plan for each of us but He leaves it up to us to choose. The biblical truth is that *your destiny is in your hands and ultimately will be determined by the decisions you make.*

At this junction in our journey, I would like to pause for a few moments and encourage you to prayerfully evaluate your personal decision-making process. You may not have it formally written out or outlined, but each of us has a process we normally go through to make decisions, especially the more important ones. Review your life through the lens of absolute honesty and ask yourself how you got to where you are today.

You are *where* you are and *who* you are because of the decisions that you have made in the past. Each of us develops a personal belief system as we grow into adulthood. We may not acknowledge this belief system, but it exists. The principles by which we live come out of this belief system. A *principle* is defined as a conviction or value that comes from our personal belief system that is used as a guide in making decisions.

In America we seem to have lost our moral compass, and many have developed their personal beliefs based on a so-called free society that teaches whatever we desire, we should be able to have. It is very popular today for young couples to live together before marriage because not only is it accepted but it is considered the smart thing to do in view of the high divorce rate. Many Christians ignore the principles taught in the Word of God and have accepted this cultural practice. They make that decision from a personal belief system based on cultural influences rather than on God's Word. Therefore, they make decisions based on *principles* contrary to the principles that govern the kingdom of God. Every decision that we make will be made based on the principles that we choose to live by, and every decision will have a consequence, either good or bad. That is why it is so important that we prayerfully consider how we make decisions and clearly define our belief system.

If you will look closely at some of the major decisions that you have made in your life, you probably will discover that in most situations you made decisions based on your feelings in that moment. If so, you are perfectly normal. Because our physical senses are so strong, we are often influenced more by them than by reason. The common result is that most of us make decisions based on *feelings* rather than *fact*. Sometimes our feelings are correct, but in many situations in which we find ourselves our emotions can cloud the truth thus resulting in poor decisions. Poor decisions are also made when we are guided by the wrong principles. Good decisions are made when we are guided by the right principles taught in God's Word, the Bible.

In the previous chapter I discussed with you the importance of discipline if you are to achieve positive change in your life. Discipline and self-control are major components in your decision-making process if you desire positive results. Through discipline and self-control you can learn how to *respond* rather than to *react* in any circumstance regardless of how emotional it may be. Note the differences between these two actions and you will understand how important self-control is to the decision-making process.

Reacting	*Responding*
Based on feeling	*Based on reasoning*
Based on circumstances	*Based on knowledge*
Based on 1ˢᵗ impressions	*Based on facts*
a. what we perceive	*a. what we know*
b. past experiences	*b. reality*
c. tunnel vision	*c. sees the whole picture*
Often results in negative behavior	*Normally produces positive results*

Learning to respond (think) before you react (act) is an acquired skill that takes a lot of work and practice. It will never be automatic but it can be achieved if you learn how to discipline yourself. As believers in Jesus Christ we must learn how to be governed by our faith rather than by our feelings. Please understand that I am not suggesting that you ignore your feelings. Our Father created us emotional beings and our feelings are extremely important. Simply put though, we can learn how to control our feelings by our faith, which will result in producing a positive response as opposed to an improper reaction.

Before closing this segment, I would like to suggest a couple of practical steps that I personally use to bring my emotions under control when I sense they are getting out of hand. I have to admit that they are not foolproof, and because of my humanness, just like you there are times that I fail. However, these simple exercises *can* work if you are willing to practice them.

First, learn your boiling point. The next time you find yourself losing control, take note of just how far you can be pushed. Identify what I call the "hot buttons" people push that irritate you the most. In identifying your breaking point, you can learn how to step out of the situation for a few moments to maintain control.

Secondly, I have learned the enormous value of developing personal focus statements to reel in my emotions in any given situation. The two questions I asked you to ask yourself earlier, *Why do I feel the way I feel? Why do I do what I do?* are my main focus statements. I find myself using them almost every day. When I sense myself reacting to a situation, I have trained cmyself to pause and ask one or both of these questions as a focus statement. This immediately causes me to stop and thoughtfully consider my response rather than reacting to my feelings. Another good question that can bring you back to reality is the question, *How important is it?* Most of the time the things that anger us are not really that important when we put the issue in context. Pausing to think about what is really important will calm you down and help you respond more appropriately. This takes discipline and practice, but it becomes easier the more you do it. I suggest that you develop two or three focus statements that work for you and try it for a month; you will notice the difference it will make.

Now that you understand how important decisions are and the overall impact they have in our lives, the next thing that you will want to do is to develop your own personal *decision-making process*. I suggest that you take some time to reflect on the way you usually make decisions. This will require complete honesty and a lot of thought, but it will help you clarify the weak areas and give you some direction in establishing a process that is both practical and workable.

I am going to share my personal decision-making process with you so that you can use it as a blueprint to build your own. Understand that this is a very personal matter and what works for one will not necessarily work for all. Individualize your plan to suit your own personality and temperament. Developing and following a decision-making plan will enable you to make good decisions by putting everything in perspective. I have developed a process that involves seven steps.

My Personal Decision-Making Process

1. Gain information / look for the big picture

2. Identify the problems

3. Consider the current circumstance

4. Explore all options

5. Make the decision

6. Develop a plan

7. Evaluate

As we approach the end of this segment of our journey, I need to discuss an uncomfortable subject, but one of great importance if we are to finish the course. How do we survive poor decisions? All of us have made them and probably will again. I suspect that many of you are regrettably living right now with the consequences of past bad decisions. Life at times can be very tough but I can assure you that you *can* survive and get back on the right track. Let me suggest four steps that you need to take if you are to survive.

The first step is to *face it.* By that I simply mean that you have to be big enough to admit that you have made a mistake. Stop the blame game and take ownership of your life. Blaming others is only an excuse that will *always get you what you've always gotten.* Break the endless cycle by confessing your wrong, truly repenting, and prayerfully asking your Father God to help you into step two.

Once you have faced it, seek ways to *fix it.* Sometimes the damage may be irreparable, but seek forgiveness from God and those whom you have hurt. Be willing to do whatever you can to make it right. If you have lied, reveal the truth; if you have stolen, work out a payment plan and make restitution; if you have hurt an individual or company, apologize in person or in writing. Whatever you may have done, if you pray and seek the wisdom of your heavenly Father, He will show you how to correct it if it can be corrected. If it can't be fixed, then humble yourself before God and ask for strength to take step three.

Forget it. That's right—just forget it. I know many people will not let you forget, they will keep a detailed journal and hold your sins against you for the rest of your life—but God doesn't. Because of the cross, He has already forgiven you and will enable you to go on in spite of your mistakes. In Him you can find complete forgiveness and an opportunity for a fresh start. When you understand this, you are ready for the final step four.

Focus on the future, not the past. *Don't let your past destroy your future.* You can not only recover, but you can find true peace and happiness. Learn how to live in God's amazing grace that comes from His unconditional love for you. He will not hold your sins against you if you truly repent (read Ps. 103).

Life is a growing process. The longer we live, the more experiences we have, the more developed our life skills become. Learn from your mistakes and don't repeat them. Just a closing thought for your meditation: Sometimes in life we make the right decisions; however, sometimes we just have to make our decisions right.

Session 2
Journal Worksheet

1. Write Joel 3:14.

_____

_____

_____

_____

_____

_____

_____

_____

_____

_____

2. Decisions have _____.

3. Your destiny is in _____ hands.

4. Briefly summarize your *current* decision-making process:

_____

_____

_____

_____

5. Most of us make decisions based on _____ rather than _____.

6. What is the major difference between *reacting* and *responding*?

_____

_____

_____

_____

7. List two of your personal focus statements.

1. _____

_____

_____

_____

2. _____

_____

_____

_____

8. List the four steps to survive poor decisions

1. _____
   _____

2. _____
   _____

3. _____
   _____

4. _____
   _____

9. What is the most important lesson you learned from this chapter?

_____
_____
_____
_____

10. Personal reflection/prayer focus. What decisions do I need to make right?

_____
_____
_____

Chaplain Larry Briggs

Therefore shall a man leave his father and mother and be joined to his wife, and they shall become one flesh. (Gen. 2:24 NKJ)

And the Scripture was fulfilled which says, "Abraham believed God, and it was accounted to him for righteousness." And he was called the friend of God. (James 2:23)

Cultivating Positive Relationships

The wholeness of life is determined by our relationships. I encourage you to pause for a few moments and reflect upon your life up to this point. You are where you are and you have become the person that you are by the powerful influence of the people with which you have chosen to associate. The old adage, "birds of a feather flock together" is a certain truth that applies to each of us. We become like the people we hang with.

This principle should motivate us to take a long hard look at who we have become and, more importantly, who influenced us the most. As our focus texts indicate, *relationship* is an intricate theme throughout the Bible, in both the Old and New Testaments. We have been created in the image of God as tripartite beings (body, soul, and spirit) and as such we have been created with a need to love and to be loved. We spend most of our time and energy in life searching for meaningful relationships that can fulfill this basic need.

God has revealed Himself to us as our heavenly *Father*. We are a part of His family, and the concept of relationship is found on almost every page of the Bible. He called Abraham a friend, and His deepest desire is to have a personal, intimate relationship with each one of us. He made this possible by sacrificing His only son on the cross, thus making it possible for us to know Him even as He knows us.

The tragedy of our generation is found in the reality that thousands attend church every Sunday, worshipping a God through a religion they don't even know. Jesus did not come to earth to start a *religion*. He came to reveal His Father to us (John 1:1, 14) that we might enter into a *relationship* with Him.

An added truth we fail to comprehend is that ultimately our earthly relationships are determined by our relationship with God or the lack thereof. Our relationship with God can be greatly influenced, even altered, by our earthly relationships. Therefore, if we are to cultivate good and lasting relationships we need to see the whole picture and cultivate our relationships based on the biblical teaching of our being created as a tripartite being. Positive relationships don't just happen, they must be cultivated and intentionally maintained by each person involved. We all need family and friends to provide for the physical and emotional support our lives requires, but only God can meet our spiritual need. He has already done so by way of the cross. However, it is our decision whether or not to enter into a close, personal relationship with Him by receiving Christ into our hearts and thereafter living according to His Word.

Now we will come to an understanding of how to develop those good and godly relationships. Our first step will be to go all the way back to creation and try to understand that as tripartite beings we experience relationships in three dimensions:

Man/Woman to God (spirit)	=	spiritual intelligence/ relationship
Man/Woman to self (soul)	=	emotional intelligence/ relationship
Woman/Man (body)	=	physical intelligence/ relationship

The natural flow of development in creation is that we first come to know God, then ourselves, and finally one another. I have come to believe that when this natural flow is disrupted, we become confused and our relationships fail us. I don't believe that a person can really come to know and like himself without knowing the God who created him or her. In the same respect, if we do not know and like who we are, how can we love someone else? This truth is clearly taught in the Bible in both the Old Testament (Lev. 19:18) and by Jesus in the New Testament (Matt. 5:43). By doing so our Father God was not only establishing a spiritual principle, but as our Creator, He speaks from a known psychological principle as well: *We cannot love others until we learn how to properly love ourselves.* The only way that we can love ourselves is to see ourselves as God sees us and to come to an understanding of His love for us (grace). Accepting this creates within us a desire to know Him and to love Him as He loves us. The natural outflowing of this will be that we will instinctively come to love others as He loves us. It really is not as complicated as it sounds, although the only way that it can become a reality in me is through the inward working of His Holy Spirit in my life. As I freely submit to the lordship of Jesus Christ in my life, His Spirit will channel that natural flow and create right relationships with Him and others. If we leave Him out of the equation, our relationships will become dissatisfying, dysfunctional, and in the end, destructive.

I suggest that we park here, take a break, and spend some time reflecting seriously on our relationship with God. If it's not right, none of our other relationships will work either. A thought for prayerful meditation: *How do your current relationships influence your relationship with Father God, and vice versa?*

Now that we have taken a moment to reflect, hopefully with a pure heart and clear mind, we can continue our journey. Understanding that we experience relationships in three dimensions gives us a good foundation upon which to build all of our relationships. Next, we need to think about the natural development of intimacy. For the purpose of our study, I define *intimacy* as a warm friendship marked by close association and/or consistent contact. Within the three dimensions of relationships, intimacy is developed in four stages:

Spiritual: cultivating a personal relationship with God.

Intellectual: sharing of thoughts, ideas, and dreams. *Emotional*: sharing of feelings and emotions.

Physical: touching with affection (both sexual and nonsexual).

It is critical that we understand the natural development of intimacy if we are to cultivate good, godly, and lasting relationships. I want you to examine the four levels of intimacy carefully and then consider some deeply troubling questions with me. Why do many of our relationships fail? Why is divorce in America (including the church) at an all-time high and now an epidemic that is out of control in our culture? How many lives have been scarred and even destroyed by a relationship that began in a fire of passion only to diminish into hatred and uncontrollable anger, resulting in physical and emotional dysfunction?

As a pastor I have been confronted with these realities more times than I want to remember. As a chaplain with the police department and in a correctional facility housing thirteen hundred-plus inmates, I see the end results every day in scenes that no one should ever see, let alone live out. The blunt truth is that what we are doing in our culture is not working. Our relationships fail us because we refuse to do it God's way. I have pondered this a lot and through prayer I believe that the Holy Spirit has given me an insight that I'd like to share with you. Although it may be painful, look back over your life and think about how most of your relationships were formed.

Here's the common scenario. We meet someone of interest, and we begin a relationship on the *intellectual* level. Not in a personal or deep sense, but we share thoughts and ideas. If the relationship develops beyond that, we will share a night out and perhaps some of our dreams. If allowed to flow in the natural course, we then will develop an *emotional* attachment. However, for many, this is where we make a major mistake. As soon as we *feel* an intellectual connection, driven by a sex-crazed culture we immediately jump into a physical relationship, totally ignoring the emotional and, more importantly, the spiritual.

The bedroom is hot and heavy, and at first we think we have found Miss America or Prince Charming. Our life has finally found its Cinderella story and now we can live happily ever after. But one day we wake up, look at our prince, and he has become a frog. Miss America no longer has the appeal that she had in the beginning, and things in the bedroom aren't that exciting anymore. We focus on all the things we don't like, become frustrated, and eventually the whole relationship dissolves, leaving us not only disappointed—again—but also devastated.

What happened? *Why didn't it work out?* Because we ignored God's natural development of intimacy. Every lasting relationship must begin on the *spiritual* level. First, I need to examine my own heart to ensure that I am in a right relationship with God. Next, I need to make sure that the person with whom I seek a relationship is spiritually compatible with my beliefs. If we do not share the same faith, our relationship will always be missing something very important.

Remember, I am not talking about casual relationships now but intimate ones. I have many relationships in life—in the community, at work, and in business—but these are just that, relationships, not friendships. Here, I'm talking about intimate friendships that chart the course of my life. That's why one of the most destructive yet successful lies Satan ever promoted is the concept of "casual sex." There is no such thing. For a sexual relationship to thrive it must be birthed out of a spiritual and emotional relationship. That's God's way, and the only way that will work.

Now you may not want to believe this but if you look closely at your life it will speak for itself. Sex is not a dirty word. God designed us as sexual beings. He created us with the desires that we have, and we experience the fullness of what He intended when we put them in the context of His plan. We are masters at destroying what God intended for our good. If you really want to experience the optimum and have the best, try it His way. Allow your relationships to develop naturally into intimacy as He planned.

To fully comprehend this concept, we need to discuss the three expressions of love and how each relates to the development of intimacy within the three dimensions of relationships. During the development of the early church, Scripture was written in the Arabic Greek language. It was a very specific, pictorial language that conveyed only one meaning for each word. Unlike the English language, words never had dual meanings. The word *love* can be found often in the Bible, but is used in three (tripartite) contexts, or with three different meanings (levels). Understanding these meanings helps us to have a better understanding of the three kinds of love that we experience in our relationships. The three biblical words used are:

Agape: used exclusively to refer to God's love (spiritual and sacrificial)

Phileo: used to define love shown family and friends (affectionate and emotional)

Eros: used to define physical love (sensual and sexual)

In the English language we use one word to describe all three. The confusion is not only in our language but more so in our basic understanding of the whole concept of love and the level upon which we establish our relationships. We need clarification not only of the specific meaning of each level, but also of how we cultivate different levels of relationships based on certain feelings and perceptions we have learned through the influence of different people in our lives. This is the heart of the *influence of character* and its role in our lives.

Agape love can only be experienced and expressed through spiritual experience and revelation. *But God has revealed them to us through His Spirit. For the Spirit searches all things, yes the deep things of God* (1 Cor. 2:10). God has revealed His love to us by the Holy Spirit who leads us into the new birth experience. When we have truly been born again, He resides within us and enables us to love ourselves and others with the same love that He has for us. *Now hope does not disappoint, because the* love of God *has been poured out in our hearts by the Holy Spirit who was given to us* (Rom. 5:5, emphasis added).

Agape is selfless, sacrificial love that can only be experienced through a personal relationship with our heavenly Father. It is spiritual in nature and can only be understood and expressed in spiritual terms. This is why I firmly believe that if our emotional (*phileo*) and physical (*eros*) relationships are to survive and become meaningful in our lives, they must be built upon the spiritual foundation of agape love. Culturally, love is defined in terms of give and take. If you love me, I will love you. If you meet my needs, I will try to meet your needs. God's love is not only a paradox to our way of thinking, but it is totally different from the world's view. Agape love is totally unconditional and is always seeking ways to give rather than looking for ways to receive. As we grow in our understanding of this kind of love by cultivating an intimate and personal relationship with Jesus, it opens our heart and aids us in expressing this level of love for each other. Only then can we develop all our relationships as Father intended.

Phileo is best understood within our modern culture as *friendship*. It is referred to as *brotherly love* in the Bible. It is the level of love upon which family relationships and true friendships exist. It is affectionate in nature and covers a multitude of needs in our lives. I have personally become convinced that true biblical marriage can only be experienced on the level of agape love where two (man and woman) become one through the miracle of God's love in us. This is the hunger and cry of every human spirit and the greatest need of each life.

However, God created us with a need for *phileo* also. We need good and positive relationships that extend beyond the covenant relationship of marriage. This is the kind of love experienced between parents and children, brothers and sisters, extended family members, and most commonly in true friendships. You might have noticed that when I refer to friendship, I emphasize *true* friends. Unfortunately, one of the painful lessons I have learned these many years in ministry is the truth that in life we assimilate many surface relationships but very few real friendships. The Bible teaches that a friend will love you *regardless* (Prov. 18:24). How many times has your heart been broken and your spirit deeply scarred because of a fractured friendship? Betrayal creates a horrible bruise that only God can heal. One of the reasons that relationships are destroyed is that we develop friendships from our cultural understanding rather than based on the principles of God's Word. We have been educated to believe that love is something that we fall into and out of. This is not so in the kingdom of our heavenly Father. Love is constant, even the phileo love expressed in friendships.

Because of the complexity of human nature and the crises that we face in life, all of us will face times of challenge in our relationships with family and friends. If our relationships are only built on mutual affection, they will fail. However, if we will allow the Holy Spirit to change the way we think, we can control the way we feel, thus building our relationships on God's kind of love (*phileo*) rather than on man's perception.

The most familiar meaning of love is the biblical expression of *eros*. From it we derive our English word *erotic*, which refers to physical or sexual attraction. Interestingly, it has the same meaning in the Bible but without our cultural interpretation and stigma. God's love is always pure. In the sixties we demanded social change and sought freedom of sexual expression. We achieved our goal and now the very freedom we sought has become a prison of lust and perversion that has eroded the moral fabric of our nation, turning us into a sex-crazed generation. We are so lust-driven that we have destroyed the sanctity of marriage and offer our own defenseless, innocent children on the altar of sexual idolatry.

Erotic love was designed and planned by our heavenly Father for the ultimate pleasure experienced between a man and his wife. It is a beautiful gift that we have defiled through a spirit of perversion that seeks to destroy everything that God created for our good. When the physical (*eros*) relationship is placed before the spiritual (*agape*), the emotional (*phileo*) is not permitted to develop, and the end result will always be the same. The fire of passion will fizzle, infidelity sneaks in, trust is destroyed, hearts are broken, and homes fall apart, leaving everyone involved in the ashes of despair and dysfunction at the ungodly altar of pleasure.

How long will we continue in the endless rut of *always getting what we have always gotten*? What will it take for us to wake up and realize that *change* is not only possible but also absolutely necessary?

Before we close this chapter, let me encourage you to pause for a time of prayer and meditation. *Another thought for prayer and meditation.* Is it possible that the root of the anger and bitterness in your heart has been planted in your life by broken relationships? Is it possible that others have a hard time loving you because you don't really love yourself? Is it possible for you to change? *Yes!* By the grace of God, you can.

This has been a very intense study. We are now at a very critical point in our journey. Let me encourage you again to embrace the pain; don't resist it. Understand that pain is a great motivator for change, and change is what we are seeking.

We need to bring this travel to a close. Our focus has been on *relationships*—understanding the importance of relationships in our lives and the influence that others can have on our destiny. Let me conclude this segment of our journey by suggesting some practical truths that are necessary to cultivate good, godly, and lasting relationships. Whether it is a marriage, a family relationship or a true friendship, there are four ingredients necessary for the success and satisfaction that we all need and desire.

For a relationship to thrive and become meaningful it must first be built on the foundation of *trust.* Trust is defined as being faithful at all times and in every situation. No relationship or friendship can survive without it. We must understand its importance and know that it does not come easily. It is birthed out of commitment and comes only as we prove to be a person worthy of its virtue.

It is developed through difficult times and is matured in the complexity of crisis in our lives. Just as fire purifies, the difficulties of life are a proving ground for genuine trust in our character. If our loved ones and friends can learn to trust us in the battle, they will find it easy to trust us in all the situations we encounter. Trust is not a matter of who we are, but it will always reveal what we are. If we lie, cheat, cut corners, and manipulate others to our advantage, they will soon learn that we cannot be trusted. However, if we practice honesty in all things, own up to our mistakes even if it hurts, and always honor our word, the influence of our character will prove that we are trustworthy.

Secondly, no relationship can survive without *respect*. Respect grows out of our affection and honor of others. It is expressed in both attitude and activity. If we truly respect someone, we will always speak in terms of endearment and sincerely consider it an honor to serve them by placing their needs and desires above our own. Unlike trust, respect is not earned. It is conveyed through position and maintained by lifestyle. We are respected for both who and what we are. If we display respect for others, they will find it easier to respect us. If a relationship is to thrive and grow each person involved must learn to value the respect of the other and live a life worthy of it.

Thirdly, the glue that cements a relationship is a spirit of *mutuality*. By mutuality I mean the shared reciprocal affection for fellowship between two persons. Simply put, it means that we like each other and enjoy being together. It's a two-sided friendship in which both desire the company of the other. Love, by its very nature, demands a response and will fade in the absence of one. Although agape is unconditional, in all of our earthly relationships there must exist a common interest. A friendship cannot be forced. Many have experienced deep hurt resulting in a damaged self-esteem due to the rejection of someone they desired a relationship or friendship with who did not share the same desire.

This would be a good place to insert a thought for meditation that could be a catalyst for change. Most of us by human instinct judge others from our first impression upon meeting them. If they "measure up" and meet our self-imposed criteria for a good person, we proceed to make friends with them. However, if there is something about them with which we are uncomfortable, we tend to pass them over with a few niceties and go on our way with no thought of cultivating a relationship. I wonder how many potential friends we have missed because we have misjudged by first impressions. Regardless of painful experiences in the past, we need to maintain an open heart and mind and discipline ourselves not to be governed by first impressions alone. Mutuality is not something that we can force, but it can be nurtured through self-control and a right spirit.

Lastly, all relationships must have clear *communication* in order to survive. All four of these ingredients are necessary and important, and I hesitate to classify one above the other, but communication is essential. Actually, I probably should devote an entire chapter to this issue, but for the sake of time and space let me summarize it here with a simple overview. I define communication as being the *clear* exchange of ideas, information, feelings, and personal perceptions between two or more individuals. Most of us assume that when we talk, others hear and understand what we are saying. This is not always true. Talking alone does not constitute communication. Listening is a major component of communication. Just because someone hears me speak does not necessarily mean they heard what I intended to say. For communication to be effective we need to learn how to listen as well as how to speak properly. Everything that is said to me is filtered through my own myriad of emotions and thoughts that have been developed in my lifetime by my unique experiences.

Let me illustrate. As a police chaplain I regularly ride along with officers in the field during their regular shift. This enables me to see firsthand what they encounter and affords me the opportunity to identify with them, thus creating a platform for personal ministry to them. Over the years I have been greatly blessed with many friends gained through this ministry. It also gives me a unique perspective in my ministry as a corrections chaplain.

Recently on such a ride-along, the officer that I was with was called to a crisis situation where a young black man was running around his front yard brandishing a .45 caliber pistol, threatening to kill himself. Upon arrival, the officer assessed the situation and immediately called for backup. We positioned ourselves behind the police cruiser for safety and attempted to establish communication with the individual. I had been in similar situations before and knew that communication was critical for a positive conclusion to this crisis. The young man was incoherent, confused, and obviously delusional.

In a matter of minutes two units arrived to assist. As I continued trying to establish a conversation with the man, the other officers secured the neighborhood and called the crisis hotline for intervention. It is not uncommon in such circumstances for the presence of police, especially in multiple units, to add to the frustration of the victim involved. I noted that this particular young man grew even more agitated, and it appeared as if he was truly going to hurt himself and possibly others as well. Crouching behind the cruiser's door, I whispered a prayer asking the Holy Spirit to help us help him. Quietly but very forcefully, the Holy Spirit suggested that I look around me and listen carefully to the young man. He was muttering incoherently but I could hear him repeating the same thing over and over. "They are going to kill me, they are going to kill me." As I looked around something dawned on me that I had not noticed before. All the officers who had responded were by coincidence white.

Immediately I began to understand our dilemma. I suggested to the officer in charge that we call in a black officer for assistance and hold down until he arrived. Shortly one of our black female officers responded, and within minutes she was in conversation with the young man. She was able to gain information that enabled us to contact the man's sister, and within the hour the situation was under control with no one being hurt.

Afterward we learned that the young man was suffering from a negative reaction to a new medication that had been prescribed for bipolar manic depression and paranoia. His mental illness had led him to believe that all white people hated him and were out to get him whenever possible. I was unable to communicate effectively with him because everything that I said was being filtered through his misconstrued thinking that I wanted to harm him because I was white.

Now, I realize that in everyday normal conversations life is not this dramatic, but it does bring up a point that we need to understand. Communication is an acquired life skill that must be developed. Never assume that you are being heard just because you are talking, and always take definitive measures to listen when others are speaking. Listen with your heart and mind as well as your ears. Communication is not complete until there has been a *clear* exchange between all parties involved. Communication is not only a vital ingredient in the recipe for a good relationship, but in the end our communication skills can greatly enhance our relationships or they can destroy them.

A concluding thought for prayerful meditation. Intimate personal relationships with family and friends are basic needs that each of us have. Remember—good relationships don't just happen. They are experienced in three dimensions through our understanding of the natural development of intimacy and cultivated through our understanding of the three expressions of love. By following God's plan we can enjoy the happiness and fulfillment that we both need and deserve.

Session 3
Journal Worksheet

1. Write the two focus Scriptures.

    1. _____
       _____
       _____
       _____

    2. _____
       _____
       _____
       _____

2. Define *tripartite being* as taught in the Bible.

    _____
    _____
    _____
    _____
    _____
    _____
    _____

_____

_____

_____

_____

_____

_____

_____

_____

_____

_____

3. Discuss the difference between *religion* and *relationship* as taught in this chapter.

_____

_____

_____

_____

_____

_____

_____

_____

_____

_____

4. How did God provide for our need for a spiritual relationship?

_____

_____

_____

_____

5. List the three dimensions that we experience in relationships.

1. _____

_____

2. _____

_____

6. List the four stages in the development of intimacy.

1. _____

2. _____

3. _____

4. _____

7. In your own words, briefly discuss why so many relationships fail.

_____

_____

_____

_____

_____

_____

_____

_____

_____

_____

8. List and define the three expressions of love.

1. _____

_____

_____

_____

2. _____

_____

_____

_____

3. _____

   _____

   _____

   _____

9. List the four ingredients of a good relationship.

   1. _____

   2. _____

   3. _____

   4. _____

10. Briefly discuss the two major components of communication.

   1. _____

      _____

      _____

      _____

   2. _____

      _____

      _____

      _____

11. Personal reflection/prayer focus: What relationships do I need to repair? What can I start doing to make my relationships better?

_____

_____

_____

_____

_____

_____

_____

_____

_____

_____

_____

_____

_____

_____

_____

_____

_____

_____

_____

_____

_____

_____

_____

A Final Observation

Let me be the first to congratulate you for completing this journey of self-evaluation. Having taken this journey myself, I know at times it was painful. Seeing yourself as you really are is not a pleasant experience. However, the end results can be very powerful if you allow the Holy Spirit to complete His work in you.

Before you close the book and move forward in the understanding you have gained through this experience, let me encourage you to take a few days to prayerfully reflect on what you have encountered. Knowledge is wonderful, but it is of no use unless you put into practice what you have learned. James admonishes us not to be "hearers only" (James 1:22). Ask your heavenly Father to give you the strength to acknowledge what needs changing in your life and then pursue that change with all of your heart.

It is my sincere prayer that this will prove to be a life-changing experience for you as you seek true freedom. I know as you "draw nigh to God" that He will draw near to you (James 4:8), and in Him alone you will discover you are *free indeed*!